Chesters Roman Fort

NORTHUMBERLAND

J S JOHNSON MA, DPhil, FSA
Principal Inspector of Ancient Monument

Set among the ancient wooded valleys of Northumberland, the fort at Chesters is the best preserved example of a Roman cavalry fort in Britain. It was one of a series of permanent troop bases added to Hadrian's Wall soon after the Wall was first built in AD122–23. It seems to have been occupied for nearly three centuries, with several changes of garrison during that time.

The substantial visible remains include the famous bath house, outside the fort itself, where the underground heating system can be clearly seen. Beyond the river are the remains of the Roman bridge which carried Hadrian's Wall across the Tyne. A collection of Roman sculpture, gathered from many different sites along the Wall, is on display in the museum.

ENGLISH HERITAGE · LONDON

Contents

presumed site of milecastle 28

turret 27b

B 6319

Visible remains
Buried remains
Modern buildings

| 0 | | | | 500 m |
| 0 | | | | 1500 ft |

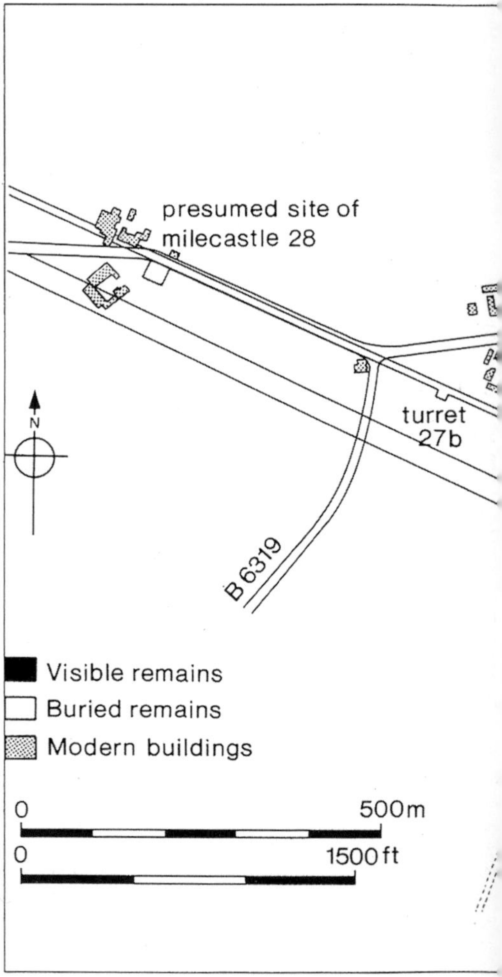

Published by English Heritage,
1 Waterhouse Square, 138-142 Holborn, London EC1N 2ST
Copyright © English Heritage 1990
First Published 1990, reprinted 1995, 1998, 1999, 2001, 2004, 2005, 2007
Printed in England by Matthews The Printers Ltd
C70   04149, ISBN 1 85074 307 X
Visit our website at www.english-heritage.org.uk

50% recycled
This book is printed
on 50% recycled paper

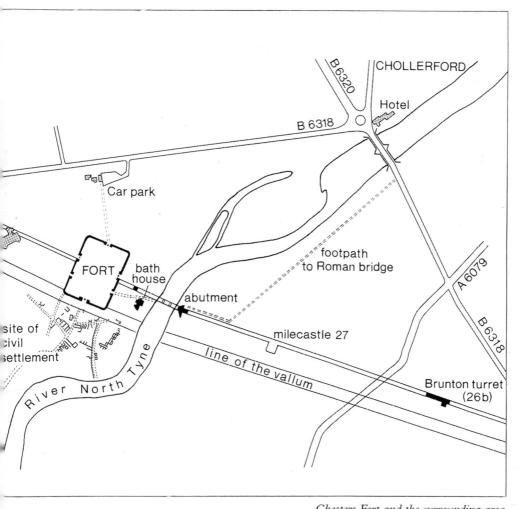

Chesters Fort and the surrounding area

Roman forts throughout the empire evolved to a very similar pattern, and Chesters, reconstructed here in a drawing by Alan Sorrell, was no exception. In plan, they had an outline rather like a playing card, rectangular with rounded corners. Two gates midway along the short sides were linked by a main street, and there were two gates, main and subsidiary, in each of the long sides. In the central area of the fort were administrative buildings, including a headquarters building and the commanding officer's house. On either side was accommodation for the troops, their mounts, and stores. This basic layout is reflected in the plan of Chesters (see page 6), though the complete plan is not exposed.

Tour of the Fort and Bath House

Orientation

Visitors to Chesters today approach the fort and Hadrian's Wall from the north – an area which in Roman times was not enclosed within the frontier. The path leading across the field from the museum and ticket office aims straight for the fort's north gate, and the first element of the fort you encounter is that portion (approximately a third of its area) which projects beyond the line taken by the Wall. The Wall itself is no longer visible in this area, but to the left it descended Brunton Bank, and ran across the fields before crossing the Tyne. Away to the right it climbed steadily, passing beneath where one wing of Chesters House now stands, aiming for Limestone Corner and the central sector of the Whin Sill.

As you approach the wicket gate, the full length of the north front of the fort can be appreciated as a low hump or plateau about 130 metres (426ft) long, which represents its full width, and is formed by the now completely buried remains of the fort wall and earth rampart backing it. A clump of trees (half right) marks the approximate position of the west side of the fort, and, further off, a

This aerial view shows the visible remains of Chesters Fort looking north, a similar angle to the reconstruction drawing opposite. (Northumbria Airfotos)

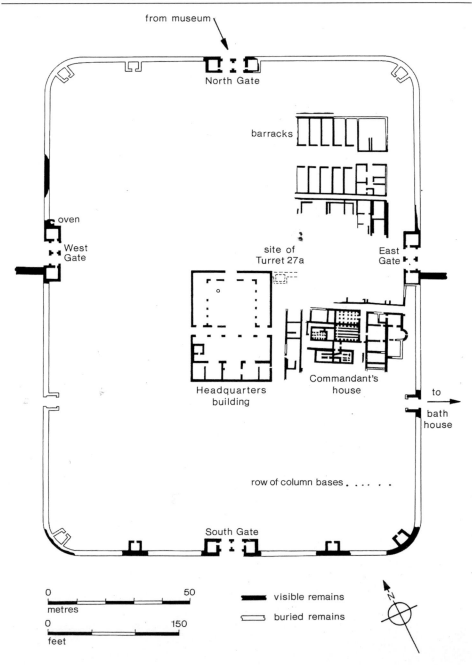

Plan of the visible remains of Chesters Fort. It is useful to compare this with the typical plan of a Roman fort (see page 40).

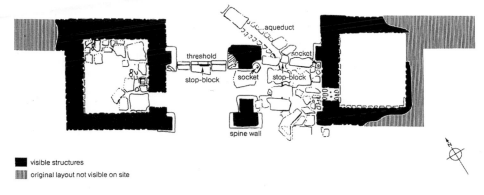

The north gate

large tree stands on the fort's south-west corner. The fort's overall length, front to back, is about 175m (574ft), and it covers an area of 2.3ha (5.7 acres).

The fort lies on a slight plateau, raised above the flood-level of the river, but within 100 metres of it. This area is now parkland surrounding Chesters House, but in the Roman period, with the fort bustling with activity, and an expansive civilian settlement sprawling outside its south gate and towards the river, the scene would have been very different. Aerial photographs show how considerable was the spread of Roman settlement around the fort, covering an area much larger than that to which visitors have access.

Only the fort itself and a small area between it and the river is in the care of English Heritage. Within a boundary fence there are slighter wire enclosures whose purpose is to keep stock out of the areas where there are exposed remains. These barriers can contribute to the visitors sense of fragmentation of the site. It is important to remember, however, that in the Roman period all the area within the fort, both where there are exposed buildings and where there is grass, would have been covered with roads and masonry or timber structures. It was a

busy, peopled and possibly crowded place, quite different from the parkland landscape of today.

North gate and north rampart

The north gate (*porta praetoria*) lay at the centre of the fort's north rampart. Its plan – a dual portalled entrance flanked by small guard-rooms – is repeated at all the site's main gateways (see page 20). This is perhaps less clearly appreciable at the north gate than at the others, for its remains are more fragmentary. The entrance passages, slightly recessed from the front face of the fort wall, can be more easily identified.

This building originally provided a dominant feature within the fort's north wall, itself 5 or 6 metres (17–20ft) in height. It would have been 10 metres (33ft) or more high, with a pair of flanking towers above the guard chambers which lay on either side of a central upper chamber above the roadways, at the height of the rampart walk. At road level, the gate was pierced by a pair of round-headed arches each blocked by a pair of stout oak gates. Only fragmentary traces remain of the central pillar of masonry which divided the two carriageways, and the front thresholds and stop-blocks which prevented the doors swinging outwards. Holes to accommodate the iron pivots on which the gates turned can still be seen tucked into the corners of the gate thresholds; these are in places accompanied by crudely chiselled, curved slots which allowed the heavy gates to be eased in or out of position.

Little can be said of the history of the gate, because here, as elsewhere at Chesters, there are problems of interpretation caused both by John Clayton's excavation in the nineteenth century (see pages 42–4) and by the presence of at least two different road levels within the east and west gate portals. The west gate portal was blocked in the Roman period but the blocking was removed by Clayton when he excavated the site: the fact that the threshold visible now is hardly worn at all by the passage of traffic suggests that the gate was blocked soon after its construction. In the other portal, however, there is no sign of blocking, but the level of the threshold and stop-blocks has been raised by about 40cm (16in), suggesting that at some date the road surface through the gate was renewed. This would have had the effect of decreasing, though probably not seriously impairing, the headroom through the gate passage. Evidence from the other gates at Chesters suggests that by the time of the abandonment of the fort, so many of the other gate passages had been blocked that this was the only one projecting north of the Wall left open.

Underlying the eastern portal, a narrow channel flanked by stones set on edge and capped by further flat stones, in places missing, is probably part of the aqueduct system which supplied the fort. Where water was brought from is not known, but it is clear that a more major supply came in at the west gate.

It is recommended at this point that you resist the temptation to examine the nearest enclosure, containing remains of the fort's barrack blocks, but instead turn right, and follow the course of the north-west angle of the ramparts round to the west gate.

West gate

Better preserved than the north gate, the west gate (*porta principalis sinistra*) also opens out north of Hadrian's Wall, a small fragment of which can be seen striking off westwards from its south guard tower. It is of similar dual carriageway plan: the central spur of masonry which divided the gate portals is more easily visible than at the north gate, and the walls of the guardchambers are several courses of masonry higher. The thresholds and stop-blocks of both carriageways are easily seen, and the pivot-holes in the angles between the guardchambers and the thresholds retain traces of their original iron lining.

When the gate was excavated by John Clayton, there were blocking walls, since removed, at both ends of the gate passages. Neither of the gate-sills exposed today shows any sign of wear, suggesting that the gate was blocked soon after its construction. Why this should have been so has never been satisfactorily explained, and Clayton's removal of the blockings, preventing any further examination of them or of any dated material they may have contained, means that there is little prospect of fresh light being shed on this problem.

Within the northern guardchamber is a stone platform which may have supported a large water tank fed by an aqueduct bringing water to the fort from the western (uphill) side. From here, the highest point on the site, a distribution system could have supplied water to those

Inscription recording the bringing of water to the fort by the second wing (Ala) of Asturian cavalry

parts of the fort which required it, and, ultimately, to the bath house lower down nearer the river. An aqueduct is known to have been constructed by the regiment *Ala II Asturum* under the governor Ulpius Marcellus, and these may be its remains. The inscription recording this, however, was found face down – not in its original position – in the carriageway of the subsidiary east gate at the opposite side of the fort.

In the angle formed by the wall of the fort and the north guardchamber lies an oven. Here and at other forts on the Wall, the area of the rampart was often used for bakehouses, perhaps to lessen the risk of sparks from the ovens setting fire to other nearby buildings.

Southern part of the fort

South rampart
The south-west angle tower, tucked into the curvature of the fort wall, lies under a large tree and has been all but obliterated by the roots. The curve of the fort wall appears from beneath the tree to begin the course of the south rampart. Here, although the fort wall itself is only visible in places, a complete run of interval

tower, south gate, interval tower and south-east angle tower can be seen, some standing to a considerable height and demonstrating the extent to which Roman occupation and the levelling of the site to form parkland have deeply buried the remains, particularly towards the south-east corner.

The south gate
The south gate (*porta decumana*) merits particular attention. Similar in most respects to the other main gates, it had two portals, the western of which was walled up by the Romans. Its blocking was removed by Clayton to reveal the earliest, relatively unworn, sill and threshold as well as the pivot-holes for the gates, once iron-clad. An aqueduct channel, probably on its way from the settling tank at the west gate towards the civilian settlement or the bath house, can be seen, covered with flat slabs, snaking through this portal. The other portal, which today appears cluttered with tumbled fragments of stone, was in fact the one left open. Here, as at the north gate, the roadway was raised, in this case by almost as much as a metre (39in), during the life of the gateway. Close

The south gate. The nearer, eastern portal was the one left open throughout the Roman occupation of the fort.

inspection reveals that the mass of stones apparently blocking this gate portal is topped by a series of rather crude threshold and stop-blocks, and that others bear distinctive pivot-holes, showing that despite their high level, they represent one of perhaps a succession of road resurfacings. This latest surface included two lengths of rainwater guttering, used upside-down, and later worn through. They are similar to those which can be seen elsewhere on the site, notably around the bath house.

The excavation of the east guardroom of the gate proved to be of exceptional interest, for Clayton found four separate periods of occupation separated by three layers of debris, in each case levelled up to make a new floor level. In one of these was discovered the military discharge certificate known as the 'Chesters Diploma' (see page 38).

From the south gate, the road led through the scatter of buildings of the civilian settlement which clustered around the fort. This was the main road connecting Chesters to the main Roman road system and to the Stanegate, the east–west road which ran about 3.2km (2 miles) south of Hadrian's Wall between Corbridge and Carlisle.

Internal buildings

The only visible element of the internal buildings within the southernmost third of the fort is the row of six column bases near the south-east corner. Clayton, however, discovered within this area a number of structures which have been backfilled. These included what appeared to be a pair of short granaries as well as a number of separate buildings which could have been barracks, workshops or stables, and whose plan is only imperfectly known. The visible row of column-bases appears to belong to one of these barrack-like structures, and looks similar to the row visible between the exposed pair of barracks in the northern part of the fort, though its position is not exactly the same.

Now walk along the east rampart up to the remains of the single-carriageway gateway. In Roman times this was the only gate opening out of the fort south of Hadrian's Wall towards the river and the fort bath house. In making your way down the hill to the baths after visiting this gateway, therefore, you are almost certainly tracing a route much used by the Chesters garrison.

Bath house

The fort bath house at Chesters is well sited between the fort and the river Tyne: water brought into the fort by its aqueduct system could be diverted to serve the baths, providing a constant supply for bathing and other purposes. Effluent from the baths could channel straight into the river. The remains of the baths, one of the best preserved along the line of the Wall, show their importance to the troops as well as providing for us a glimpse of the elaborate nature of the treatments available.

Like many other Roman buildings on the Wall, the baths were in use for many years, during which time they were continually modified and improved. This means that it is not always easy to unravel the complexities and nuances of purpose to which the building was put, and much of its development to its present form is poorly understood. In addition, throughout much of the building, what is ground level today was for the Romans the base of the underfloor heating system. The Roman floors were supported at a much higher level – at about the height of many of the existing walls.

The baths were first excavated in 1884–85 and then recorded in a remarkable series of photographs by J P Gibson (see page 43). These serve to show not only the state of preservation of the remains at the time of their discovery, but also the extent to which successive excavations have changed some parts of the baths in the last hundred years and more.

The bath house, seen looking west from the river bank

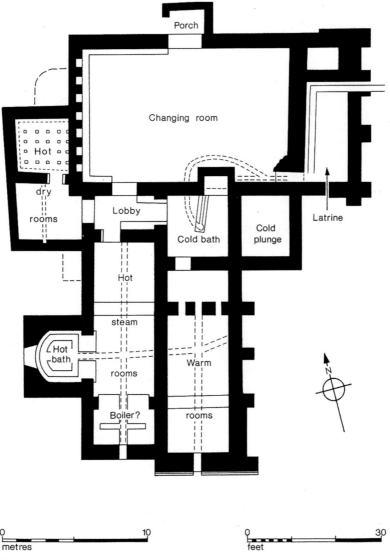

Plan of the baths

Entrance, changing room and latrine
The steps lead down to a small porch which leads into a large rectangular changing room. Observations made when parts of the bath house walls were being consolidated suggest that this room was added at a later stage to the rest of the bath house (now the hot and warm treatment rooms) south of it. If this is so, the changing room for the earlier baths may either have lain elsewhere, or may have been of timber on the site of the present room.

The changing room was probably in use for many years. The first excavations revealed a flagged floor on which stood pillar-bases for columns (or wooden pillars) to support the roof. There was an earlier floor, however, at a lower level. The evidence for this is the presence of a stone support for a bench visible at the foot of the wall containing the row of niches. The top of the bench support is at present ground level; this earlier floor must lie 0.5m (20in) below your feet.

The most obvious feature of the changing room is the row of seven niches in its west wall. Although these are sometimes interpreted as lockers for clothing or valuables, this is unlikely to be the case: apart from two large holes whose purpose is unclear, there are no holes in

The stone support for a bench at the foot of the seven niches in the changing room

This reconstruction drawing gives a general impression of how the baths may have looked in Roman times. Although some of the details are now known to be incorrect (the drawing was made in the 1950s), the drawing serves well to indicate the vaulted ceilings of the main hot treatment rooms (see page 17) and the more conventional roof of the large changing room. (Drawing by Alan Sorrell)

the stonework which could have been used to fix wooden doors to these niches, and far more than seven lockers must have been needed at a fort with between 400 and 500 men in garrison, as well as civilians in its surrounding settlement. The niches are far more likely to have contained a series of seven statues, most probably representing the days of the week – Sol (the sun), Luna (the moon), Mars, Mercury, Jupiter, Venus and Saturn. Other statues are known to have come from the bath house, including an altar to the goddess Fortuna. Her presence there suggests that men in their idle hours indulged in a light flutter or two, probably in the changing room which would thus have had a social as well as a utilitarian function.

The altar to Fortuna Conservatrix, goddess Fortuna, the protector

It is not certain where water entered the bath house, nor how it was stored. Common sense might suggest that there ought to have been a tank a little up the slope from the baths, but no trace of this has been found. Fresh cold water, however, in what must have been a constant supply, was available to flush the latrine, which lay at the river end of the changing room. A narrow doorway in the south-east corner of the changing room led to this latrine, constructed on a kind of buttressed platform. Wooden seats were suspended over the deep channel which runs round two walls of this room before disgorging through the east wall towards the river. Much of the east wall of both the changing room and the latrine

An artist's impression of the interior of the changing room, showing the bench, the lower flagged floor, the seven niches, and the steps up to the lobby leading to the heated rooms beyond. (Drawing by Frank Gardiner)

The latrine channel at the east end of the changing room

has gone, making the original arrangements at this point difficult to envisage.

Alternative treatments
The present layout of the bath house suggests that in its last phase there was a range of different treatments available to customers. One was a hot dry treatment, provided in the ante-room and the hot dry room, tucked round the corner of the changing room. From the lobby up the steps from the changing room, the bather could also go straight on into a range of hot baths and steam treatments in the hot rooms, or left into the cold bath and a series of warm rooms in a suite of rooms parallel to, but linked with, the hot bath.

Hot dry rooms
(*laconicum/sudatorium*)
Turning right out of the lobby the bather, now wearing sandals – the suspended floors would have been kept unbearably hot by the circulation of air from charcoal furnaces – first entered an ante-room where heat would begin to build up, before going through into the small hot dry room itself, marked by a stoke hole outside its wall. Here not only the floor, but also the walls were heated: here and

there traces can be seen of the iron clamps which held a thin skin of stone in place, enabling the walls to be warmed with a continual current of hot air. This treatment, something akin to a sauna, would need to be rounded off with a rapid dash back through the ante-room and the lobby to the cold plunge, to wash off the sweat and close the pores. Before following the bather (though not so precipitately), note that the floor of the hot dry room is suspended on Roman pillars; this is the level at which floors would have lain throughout the rest of the building.

The massive stone jambs of the doorway, better preserved here than anywhere else on the site, are worth noting. Threshold stones can be seen in several places on the site with characteristic grooved areas to receive the upright jambs, but this doorway (only missing its lintel) shows what has been lost elsewhere.

Cold bath (*frigidarium*)
Immediately left of the lobby lay the cold bath. This was originally an ante-room leading to a small square room towards the river, probably the cold plunge. The way in which the steps from the lobby to

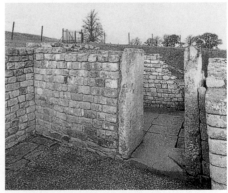

The doorway to the small hot dry room, with its well preserved stone jambs

This site of the cold plunge, with the river beyond. In the foreground is the drain which carried the run-off from the basin in the centre of the room

the cold room have worn shows that the natural tendency was for bathers to turn right on immediately entering the room. This suggests that there was some obstacle – perhaps a basin – at its centre. Slipping off his sandals, and avoiding this obstacle, the bather would plunge into the depths of the cold bath for refreshment and relief from the build-up of heat.

At a later stage it appears that the cold bath went out of use and a much smaller plunge was substituted: this lay in a corner of the cold room and encroached on the area of the changing room. The basin or douche at the centre of the cold room stayed in position: the stone which lies there at present seems to have formed some part of the run-off from the basin, It has two channels, one running under (or through) the later small bath to the latrine, the other running as if to go round it on the same route. This suggests that it was retained in use, and that the water running off from it was used to supplement water used to flush the latrine.

Warm rooms (*tepidaria*)

From the central lobby a series of steam (rather than dry) heat treatments was available in the main range of the building. Building up gradually, the first room was reached through the cold bath, by turning left out of the lobby. This seems to have acted as an ante-room to

The warm rooms looking south, showing part of the paved floor supported on pillars.

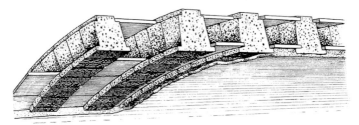

This drawing shows how the barrel vaulted ceiling of the hot rooms may have been constructed from shaped sandstone blocks and tiles. (Frank Gardiner)

the large warm room in the south-east corner of the building. Both these rooms had hypocaust underfloor heating served by a stoke hole outside their south wall and may originally have been slightly smaller than at present. At a late stage in the life of the bath house, the hypocaust heating system fell into disuse and was filled with sand.

Floor level in these rooms, however, was at least a metre higher than it is today – paved floors were supported on pillars here to allow circulation of hot air. A doorway connected the second warm room to the hot room and its hot baths: traces of its threshold can be seen in the very top of the wall between it and the hot room. The narrow opening in the south wall which can now be used to walk out of the building was in Roman times the stoke hole arch, and not a doorway.

Hot rooms (*caldaria*)

The bather who wanted immediate hot steam treatment could go straight on from the lobby through an ante-room to the hot room. Here, as in the range of warm rooms, Roman floor levels were about a metre higher than today, and further confusion is caused by the fact that all trace of the wall which once existed between the ante-room and the hot room has now gone, Both rooms were heated by

a furnace outside the south wall, where the stoke hole can still be seen.

The two steps down from the lobby to the ante room are worth a second look. They were placed there after excavation in 1885, but are elements of sandstone blocks which once formed a barrel-vaulted ceiling over at least this part of the bath house. They are similar to other blocks which can be seen piled behind the bath house west wall. It has been suggested that by combining shaped stones such as these with tiles (see above), a light and hollow ceiling could have been achieved for this suite of rooms, containing ducts for hot air, thus achieving all-round heat and cutting down

The D-shaped basin which contained the hot bath

the inevitable condensation on the walls, and allowing the actual steam treatment to be more effective.

From the ante-room the bather went on into the hot rooms, full of hot steam and in which, in a small D-shaped basin to his right, lay the hot bath. This tank, probably of lead, which has now disappeared, was supported on the masonry structure which can still be seen in this room.

The channels (which of course were below floor level) allowed hot air to circulate. Traces of the pink mortar which must have covered much of the lower parts of the walls here are visible within the D-shaped bath-annexe. At high level, there are signs of a small window with a deeply splayed sill.

At the south end of the room is a similar platform which may have held another hot bath or, perhaps more likely, supported the boiler for hot water feeding the whole of the baths. There are a number of holes in the masonry at high level in this area which may have held pipes feeding such a tank, but the original disposition at this end of the hot room cannot now be properly understood.

At their fullest extent, the baths would have required three major furnaces to be kept supplied with charcoal to build up the intense heat levels required. On a cold day at Chesters amid the impressive though ruinous remains, it is hard to imagine the levels of warmth and comfort (one might almost say discomfort) achieved within this building.

Civilian settlement

The whole area to the south and south east of the fort, and around the bath house, was covered with a scatter of buildings. As with the inside of the fort, therefore, this present-day parkland landscape must be filled in our imagination with a bustle of people and buildings, some of stone, others of timber. There would have been temples, shops,

The fort seen from the south east. Between the fort and the river, clear traces can be seen of the streets and buildings of the civilian settlement which lay outside the fort's south gate. (Cambridge University Collection)

dwellings (some possibly housing the strictly illegal wives and families of serving soldiers), small holdings, warehouses and other establishments offering goods or services of all kinds, attracted by the prospect of troops with money to spend. Further south would have lain cemeteries and possibly, on this side of the river or the other, a mill.

Traces of what lay round the baths themselves show up only indistinctly on aerial photographs. However, the street leading to the baths and to the bridge across the Tyne was probably one of the most frequented and therefore the site for much of the commercial activity. In picturing what this area was like in Roman times, we must also remember that the view to the north was cut off at this point by Hadrian's Wall itself – some 6 metres (20ft) high, and running from the fort straight down to the river, which it crossed by means of a stone bridge. This area was therefore far more enclosed, grimy, claustrophobic and smelly than one can easily imagine today.

Before retracing your steps up the hill to the fort, it is worth considering the bridge itself. Although the main visible remains of the massive bridge abutment (see page 29) lie on the other bank of the river (and can only be reached from a footpath leading off from the eastern approach to Chollerford Bridge), there was once a corresponding abutment on this bank. The course of the Tyne has shifted since Roman times to eat into the Chesters bank and only very fragmentary traces of the abutment are occasionally visible in the river bed. Some of the stone piers which carried the two successive bridges have also been located in mid stream at times when the water is low.

On your way back to the fort is a small portion of Hadrian's Wall within a fenced enclosure part way up the slope. This aims straight for the guardchamber of the fort's main east gate, and is a reminder that although we can stroll easily into the enclosure which houses the east gate and the barracks, in Roman times the Wall would have barred the way. The only way into the fort for the Romans was through the subsidiary gate; the main east gate opened out north of the Wall.

Main east gate

This is one of the best preserved fort gateways on Hadrian's Wall. Like the other main gates, it is double-portalled, with guardchambers on both sides. The central spine between the entrance passages is particularly well preserved, and parts of the rear arch survive to the level of the stone which supported the semicircular gate arch itself.

Of the three main fort gates which opened north of Hadrian's Wall, this one was perhaps of less use than the others, for movement eastwards from this point was cut off by the river. Eventually, this led to the complete blocking of the gate. The blocking, removed by Clayton when he excavated the gate, seems to have belonged to more than one stage. It is hard to tell when this happened; the apparently unworn original sills now visible are sometimes thought to indicate that the gate was walled up early in the life of the fort, but if because of its position there was little traffic through the gate anyway, this would not be conclusive.

Hadrian's Wall, progressing westwards from the river, met the fort wall at the south guardchamber. The gate itself, therefore, was built across the site of the wall ditch, which had already been dug before Chesters and most of the other forts were added to the Wall. As a consequence, the foundations of the north gate tower are much deeper than its southern counterpart.

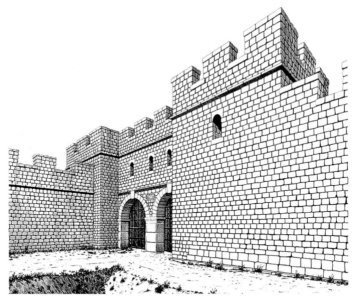

An artist's reconstruction of the exterior of the east gate. The wall to the left is Hadrian's Wall running up to the southern guardchamber. The Wall ditch (in the foreground) has had to be partially filled to provide a footing for the northern guardchamber, and to give access to the gate itself. (Drawing by Frank Gardiner)

The east gate, seen from its southern guardchamber

An artist's impression of the interior of the cross hall, looking from the north aisle just inside the main entrance from the courtyard across the body of the hall to two of the smaller rooms off its south side. The room on the left is the regimental chapel. (Drawing by Alan and Richard Sorrell)

Looking up the street which divided two of the Chesters barracks blocks. The officer's quarters lay at the far end.

picked out on one of the stones. Round three sides of this courtyard there seems to have been an open colonnade: portions of the stone guttering which took water dripping from its roofs can be seen following the courtyard's edge. Although the colonnade was doubtless also paved, no trace of this has survived.

From the courtyard and from each of the colonnades, a main opening – probably double doors – led into the rear range, a large hall set across the line of the building. Doors to east and west also allowed access to this hall from outside. The hall provided a lofty enclosed space, lit by upper-storey windows and subdivided by columns, which could be used for meetings, hearings, briefing sessions and ceremonial occasions. At one end was a platform, the *tribunal*, where the commanding officer would take his place; elsewhere within the building are traces of bases for statues and altars. The head-quarters was the seat of discipline, duty and morale, a place sacred to the garrison.

Off the south side of the hall lay a range of smaller rooms. The central one, barred off from the rest of the building by a stone screen similar to an altar-rail, was the regimental chapel. Here statues of the reigning emperor were kept, and no doubt the regimental standards too, as well as trophies or distinctions gained by the unit in garrison in the course of its history of service to the empire. The museum contains inscriptions and stone reliefs which may once have held pride of place in this room.

There were two rooms on either side of the chapel. These, little suites of offices, may have housed the records, and the clerks who organised duty rosters and pay and kept a record of equipment issued or rations supplied. The building was the administrative hub of the unit's occupancy of the fort.

It is at this point too that the massive build-up of occupation levels within the fort and the effects of levelling to create the parkland terrace can best be seen. To reach the exposed remains of the barracks in the north-east portion of the fort it is necessary to pick your way between the north gate tower and a grassy bank, perhaps 2m high, which represents the build-up in this part of the fort. This, of course, contains remains of all phases of the fort's occupation, but excavation has not taken place here.

Barracks

The remains of the barracks are of three separate buildings. All were long and narrow, and originally stretched from a road running round the interior of the fort ramparts to the main road down the centre of the fort. They therefore measured about 53m (174ft) long. At least to begin with, Chesters was a cavalry fort, and so there should have been provision within it for barracks for men and equipment (necessarily more bulky than for infantry), as well as for stables. There would also have been workshops, among which the smithy, for keeping horses well shod, would have been most important.

None of the three buildings visible today is exposed in its full length. The southern building is the most puzzling. It seems to be subdivided in a rather irregular fashion, which may indicate other, later and smaller buildings built in and around the remains of a larger one. The layout is reminiscent of the later Roman development which is known to have occurred at Wallsend and

Housesteads forts, where original long buildings (probably barracks) had smaller individual buildings – 'chalets' – put up in their place. The lack of information about the Chesters buildings makes any firm interpretation difficult: least of all what the original long building was used for.

With the two northern buildings we are on surer ground. These are a pair of barrack blocks of apparently normal pattern. Despite the fact that their full length is not exposed, they are the only regular barracks of second-century date to be seen on Hadrian's Wall (see reconstruction, page 41). They are long buildings, subdivided into smaller mess rooms for the men, facing each other across a street. At the end nearer the rampart a larger unit contained a suite of rooms for their commanding officer. It seems that a barrack block of this type was required for the 80 men of an infantry century or for the 64 men of two cavalry squadrons (allowing for all their extra equipment), but how these men were disposed within the available accommodation is not known. Since only the eastern portions of these two barrack-blocks can be seen, we can only guess whether there were eight or ten barrack rooms within each block. If ten rooms were available, the accommodation, at least mathematically, would have suited infantry better, but real-life solutions to such accommodation problems were probably rarely as neat as archaeologists' theories.

Central range

The central range of the fort contained the main administrative buildings, the headquarters, and also the house of the commandant and his staff, built to a standard affording him the luxury appropriate to his status. Before entering the gate which leads to the central building of the fort, however, it is once more worth remembering that the fort was placed on this spot as an after-thought:

Hadrian's Wall was once planned to run continuously across the centre of the fort, entering, as it were, at the east gate and going out at the west. Just to one side of the headquarters building itself, the site of one of the earlier turrets on the Wall – number 27a according to our modern numbering system – has been located by excavation. The foundations for this were laid, and perhaps some of the superstructure built, before the decision was taken to supplant it with the fort; but it had probably not been finished.

Headquarters building

The headquarters building (*principia*) is one of the most distinctive of the buildings of a Roman fort. It faced northwards, and its main entrance lay at the end of the street which led into the fort from the main north gate. This main door opens

The phallus carving set into the courtyard paving of the headquarters building

into a large open courtyard originally completely paved with large stone slabs, which survive in part. Towards the north-west corner there is an opening for a well let into the paving, and near it, a carving of a good luck 'phallus' is clearly

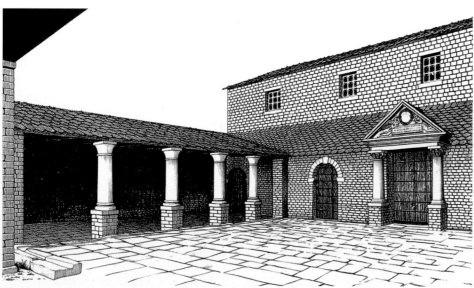

An artist's reconstructed impression of the view across the courtyard of the headquarters building. The tall building with the rectangular windows is the 'cross hall'. (Drawing by Frank Gardiner)

View from the north-west corner of the headquarters, looking across the courtyard towards the remains of the rear range. In the foreground is the well. The viewpoint is close to the artist's reconstruction opposite.

At a later stage, a part-sunken strong room (see front cover illustration) was added, reached via a flight of steps from the regimental chapel. This was discovered in 1803 and excavated in 1840, when it was found to have a large iron-bound and studded door (which unfortunately has not survived) still in place. The strong room has a ribbed roof and encroaches considerably on the small office room to its east. Either the floor level in the Roman period was considerably higher in this part of the headquarters than it is now, or the office must have gone out of use.

Commandant's house

On both sides of the headquarters lay other major buildings in the central range, though at Chesters nothing is now visible west of the headquarters. At other forts these include store buildings (granaries),

workshops or the hospital. One side of the central range, however, was normally reserved for the commandant's quarters. Because the commander of a unit of auxiliary cavalry was often a man of considerable rank and social (if not political) pretension, the quarters allotted to him and his family are not markedly different from a comfortable, well-appointed house in a Roman town in the rest of the province of Britain, if not in the Mediterranean area.

At Chesters, the area to the east of the headquarters which is occupied by the commandant's house contains one of the most complex groups of remains on the site. Immediately next to the headquarters is a long narrow building, separate from the rest, which could have been a workshop or stable. It does not appear to have had any domestic use.

Part of the bath suite attached to the east end of the commandant's house. The heated rooms project into the line of the road which led around the fort within the ramparts.

The statue of Neptune, discovered within the commandant's house

Next to this lies the house proper. This was not the earliest building on this part of the site, for excavation at selected points has revealed fragmentary traces of a completely different layout underneath. The remains now visible appear to be those of three suites of domestic rooms around a central courtyard which has increasingly been encroached on and added to during the building's use. A number of the rooms are provided with hypocausts and, at a late stage in its history, the building was extended eastwards to provide a separate small suite of baths with semicircular ends. As in the main bath block, a number of door thresholds show that the floors in this part of the building were at the level of the top of the surviving remains. The bath block extends the commandant's house into the space normally occupied by the road round the fort ramparts, and must have obstructed circulation round the fort in this area.

This completes the visit to the fort and bath house. There are two further elements of the remains at Chesters: one is the museum, and the other the remains of the Roman bridge which carried the line of the wall across the river Tyne.

Museum

The museum was completed after John Clayton's death to house and display his collection of objects from many sites on the Roman Wall which formed one of the attractions, even by 1900, to the increasing number of visitors to Wall country.

The wealth of material it contains defies brief description. The main room, entered through a small porch, is much as planned around 1900. It contains three original table cases set in its centre, and the walls are lined with stone reliefs and sculptures not only from Chesters, but also from the forts of Vindolanda, Housesteads, Carvoran and Carrawburgh, all of which belonged to the Clayton family. The layout in this main room is typical of a museum of the day, in which important pieces are cheek-by-jowl with less significant finds, arranged in no particular order.

Many of the sculptured stones referred to or pictured in this guide will be found in the museum. They include one of the finest pieces of Roman sculpture in the Hadrian's Wall area, the representation of Juno Dolichena – Juno standing on a heifer – the consort of Jupiter Dolichenus, who is portrayed standing on a bull. Another stone shows Neptune reclining: this came from the commandant's house area and may have embellished the baths.

Of particular interest among the sculptures which come from places other than Chesters are the stones from the well of Coventina at Carrawburgh. The inner (second) room of the museum contains a case of material which came from this site, but the collection includes a rather naive sculpture of Coventina herself as well as a stone which portrays three water nymphs.

Also in the inner room is a collection of military ironwork as well as the bronze *modius*, or dry corn measure, from Carvoran. Full to the brim, it holds about 11 litres (20 pints), but bears an inscription in careful lettering which defines its capacity: this states that the measure holds 17$\frac{1}{2}$ sextarii around 9.5

One of a number of dedications to the goddess Coventina, now in Chesters Museum. These were all found at Carrawburgh, the next fort along the Wall to the west, where a small spring just outside the fort was dedicated to her.

litres (17 pints). A gauge inside the brim of the vessel marking this measure may be missing.

The bronze corn measure found at Carvoran and now in the museum

Chesters Bridge

The remains of the bridge on the east bank of the river North Tyne are approached along a footpath from near Chollerford Bridge, which follows the track of a disused railway for about a kilometre. At the stile, where the path down to the river and the bridge abutment branches off at an angle, you are once again following the line of Hadrian's Wall. As you approach the river, the Wall emerges from the grass, and the massive stone blocks of the abutment of the bridge come into view.

These remains were first located in 1860. They form one of the most impressive and massive masonry structures to be seen on the Wall. A shift in the course of the Tyne has moved the river westwards about 20m (66ft), completely covering or sweeping away much of the west abutment, on the fort side of the river. This left the eastern abutment high, if not always dry, on the other bank.

The first bridge

There were at least two bridges on this spot. The first, less massive than its successor, was probably contemporary with the construction of the Wall in AD122–4. Excavation has located its eastern end directly underneath the tower which now stands on the large later abutment. It crossed the river on a series of at least eight hexagonal stone piers about 4m (13ft) apart: the first of these (from the east) can be seen where it has

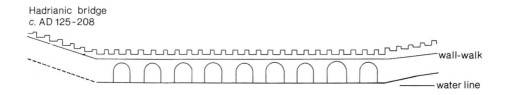

Hadrianic bridge
c. AD 125-208

wall-walk

water line

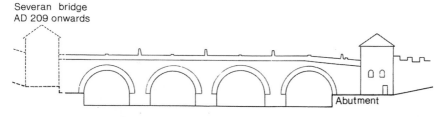

Severan bridge
AD 209 onwards

Abutment

These artist's sketches compare the elevations and sizes of the two successive bridges which crossed the Tyne at Chesters. The Hadrianic bridge (above) was on a far smaller scale than its early third-century replacement (below).

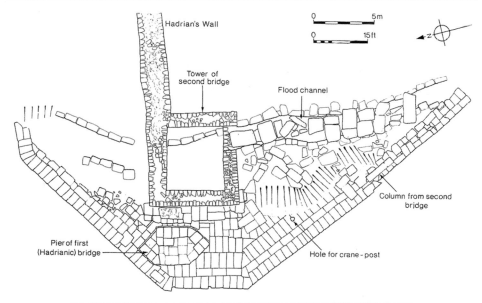

Hadrian's Wall

Tower of
second bridge

Flood channel

Column from second
bridge

Pier of first
(Hadrianic) bridge

Hole for crane - post

0   5m

0   15ft

*Top: plan of the remains of the east abutment of the Roman bridge at
Chesters which carried Hadrian's Wall across the river Tyne. The
photograph beneath shows the remains from the same angle.*

An artist's view of the second, early third-century bridge, viewed from downstream. Note the positioning of the columns on the bridge parapets: the large column now lying on the abutment (see opposite) is one of these. (Frank Gardiner)

been incorporated into the stonework of the later abutment. The overall length of the bridge between abutments was 61m (200ft).

The width of these piers suggests that the bridge was intended to convey a structure 3.1m (10 ft) wide – the width of the Broad Wall in this area – and that it therefore carried Hadrian's Wall across the river with a series of small stone arches. The masonry appears to have been plain but substantial, and the surviving hexagonal pier bears traces of dovetail cramps of iron set in lead which would have held the stones tightly together.

The second bridge

The second bridge, which accounts for much of the masonry presently visible on the site, was far more massive. Its construction seems to have followed a period when silt and gravel were deposited on the east bank, and when a major inundation had perhaps destroyed the easternmost arch of the earlier bridge.

There are signs that the river was already shifting its course westwards, a process which has continued since Roman times.

The new eastern abutment was a far more massive affair than before, with splayed wing walls both north and south of the bridge's actual line. This abutment, its massive rectangular stones lifted into place using the lewis holes which are a feature of their upper surface, were held together with long iron ties channelled into the masonry to reinforce the front face. From this solid abutment there sprang an elegant bridge with four arches supported on three substantial river piers, 10.5m (34ft) apart. Its overall length was 57.5m (189ft). This was more massive than the previous bridge, and was intended to take a road carriageway; a ramp against the south face of Hadrian's Wall in this area led up to the level of the bridge, which was entered through the tower placed at the end of Hadrian's Wall.

Much of the decorated stonework on the site belongs to the superstructure of this bridge. Few voussoirs (wedge-shaped

An artist's view of the same bridge, viewed from upstream. There are cutwaters on this side, the central one of which may have been a shrine. (Frank Gardiner)

stones from arches) have been found, but there is sufficient other evidence in the form of cornice blocks, grooved to take vertical parapet slabs, and angled mouldings, to show that the bridge was of stone. The massive column which lies on the abutment bears a moulding at its foot, and was one of at least four which stood at intervals across the bridge, interrupting the parapet.

This second bridge seems to date from the early third century. There is no evidence for any further repair or alteration to the bridge after that date, though later the south wing of the abutment was extended and the water channel – perhaps for flood relief – was forced through the base of the tower above the abutment. It seems unlikely that this water channel served a mill on the site of the tower, as has sometimes been supposed, though there may have been a mill slightly further downstream.

The lower part of the column, originally part of the bridge parapet, now lying on the east abutment.

The Romans in the North

The expansion of Rome

Roman armies, carrying out the orders of the Emperor Claudius, invaded southern Britain in AD43. Ever since Julius Caesar's brief expeditions into Britain in 55 and 54 BC, Rome had enjoyed relatively peaceful contacts through trade and diplomacy with the independent Celtic tribes and rulers within the island. However, after the expulsion of a prominent Roman sympathiser, and perhaps other signs that open hostilities were planned, it became necessary for Claudius to act. His arrival on the imperial throne, an unlikely survivor from the political mayhem in the wake of Augustus and Tiberius, needed to be marked by positive action to prove his worth in the minds of the Roman senate and people. The invasion of Britain, new territory for Rome, was begun.

The progress of Roman control was rapid at first, but after initial military success came a period of consolidation, accompanied by the occasional need to root out trouble, for example the revolt of Boudicca in AD60–61. By the 70s, attention was turning towards the north. Fortresses for Roman legionary troops were established at Chester and York, ready to form a springboard for further military advances northwards. By AD78, when a new governor, Gnaeus Julius Agricola, was appointed to the province, much had already been done to subdue the Brigantes in northern England, and a network of forts established over much of their territory quickly completed the annexation of this area.

By AD85, Agricola's armies had carried out a series of brilliant campaigns in Scotland, culminating in a battle at Mons Graupius. It seemed that the conquest was complete, and forts and bases were established over much of lowland Scotland. But the peoples of the highlands proved less amenable to the foreign presence of Rome. Gradual and insistent pressure on the Roman forces at the hands of these folk, coupled with the need for troops to be deployed on other frontiers, led to a planned withdrawal from Scotland by Roman troops, involving evacuation, abandonment and the dismantling of existing forts. By the very first years of the second century, Roman presence in Scotland was minimal, and the main concentration of troops and their bases lay on and to the south of the line of the Stanegate, the Roman road which linked Carlisle and Corbridge.

A number of military installations lay on and in association with this road which formed Rome's northern frontier at this date. Indeed, in origin, the Latin word for a frontier, *limes*, means just such a track as this, and the association of forts, smaller fortlets, and watchtowers along its length shows that the Roman military commanders had well appreciated the strategic importance of this cross-country route, and were prepared to defend it. The line of this road is well known in parts today: it crosses the Tyne about a mile south of Chesters near the village of Wall. Whilst its course eastwards towards Corbridge is uncertain from this point, its route westwards is followed by the minor road running through Fourstones and Newbrough towards Vindolanda. The latter site itself was established originally as one of the forts on the Stanegate system, although the fort of this phase is buried deep beneath the existing visible and later remains. The remarkable finds of writing tablets, however, and much of the rich display of finds on display at the site comes from the turf and timber fort of this date.

No major alteration other than consolidation of positions in parts of northern England, including the Lake District, took place within the reign of Trajan (AD98–117). His successor, Hadrian, who came to power in AD117, was immediately faced not only with political problems in Rome, but with military threats of some kind in Britain. These were resolved by 119, but soon afterwards, Hadrian decided to undertake a tour of his northern and western provinces. In 121, he was in Gaul and

Germany, and in the next year, he became the first Roman emperor since Claudius in 43 to visit Britain.

The building of Hadrian's Wall

There can be little doubt that the plan to establish a permanent frontier along the east–west corridor in northern England was Hadrian's, whether it was actually formulated during his visit to Britain or not. Originally, the Wall was planned as a linear barrier to run from the bridge across the Tyne at Newcastle to the Solway Firth at Bowness, a distance of 76 Roman miles (122km). This barrier, some 4.5m (15ft) high, possibly with a wall-walk and parapet on top, was

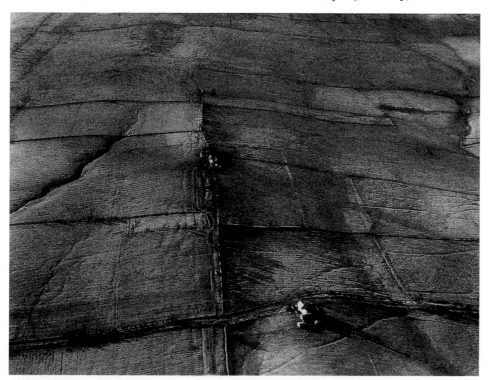

Aerial view looking west along the line of the Roman road, the Stanegate, to the west of Vindolanda fort. The road runs as an earthwork just to the left of the field walls and buildings running up the middle of the picture. (Cambridge University Collection)

A near-contemporary view, from Trajan's Column, erected in Rome in AD113, of Roman legionary troops engaged in building a turf and timber rampart. (Mansell Collection)

reinforced with regularly spaced fortlets (milecastles), marking each Roman mile length and containing virtually the only gates through the Wall, with smaller towers (turrets), two to each intermediate stretch. Construction on such a massive scale was a matter of considerable planning, and the evidence is that the builders were Roman legionary troops assisted, at least in the latter stages, by non-Roman troops from other parts of the empire (auxiliaries) and other military units. Work appears to have begun almost as soon as Hadrian left Britain in 122, and separate sections of the work were allocated to individual troop units.

Building did not begin at one end and progress steadily towards the other. The route of the Wall was carefully mapped out and some elements of the structure, including the milecastles and turrets, were built first, forming a framework onto which the linear curtain wall could later be grafted. In addition, west of the river Irthing in Cumbria, the barrier was planned to be of turf: here the turrets were stone-built, but the milecastles were of turf and timber, like the Wall itself. Conversion of this western stretch of 31 Roman miles (50km) to stone only occurred at a later stage.

While this wall was still being built, there was a change of plan. At first, the only provision for stationing men actually on the Wall, which followed a strategically favourable course normally about a mile or two north of the Stanegate track, was within the small fortlets (milecastles) attached to the Wall. Tactical planning appears to have been that troops within the bases on the Stanegate line would be used to give support where necessary. But before the linear barrier was completed, and apparently after most of the positions of milecastles and turrets had been established, the decision was taken to add eleven permanent forts to the line of the Wall. Six of these, where the terrain allowed, were placed astride the Wall, with more of their gates opening north of the Wall's line than south.

At the same time, or perhaps slightly later, the Wall was extended eastwards for about 6.5km (4 miles) from the bridge at Newcastle to a twelfth new fort at Wallsend, and a further earthwork, known as the vallum, was added south of the Wall for virtually the whole of its length. Finally, though not necessarily immediately, four more forts were either added to the curtain, or built or rebuilt nearby: unlike the earlier forts, these did not project beyond the line of the Wall, and appear to have filled particular gaps in the existing cover.

The main stages of construction of Hadrian's Wall summarised here have been mapped out by archaeological excavations and research over more than half the present century. This broad picture may in due course be sharpened up by further, more detailed research. At

An artist's reconstructed view of Brunton Turret, seen from the same angle as the photograph below. (Frank Gardiner)

Brunton Turret, no 26B, and a stretch of Hadrian's Wall. This lies about 1km (0.5 mile) east of Chesters Fort and is also in the care of English Heritage.

present, however, it appears that the eventual form of the Hadrianic frontier, with its wall, milecastles, turrets, forts and vallum, was well established by about AD130, even though further work is now beginning to show that portions of the linear barrier may not have been completed until much later.

What did the Wall achieve? It was indeed a barrier, originally probably intended as a frontier control, but once established, it may have formed more of a hindrance to Roman mobility than a positive benefit in curtailing illicit or hostile movements to the north. Why, otherwise, should troop bases so quickly have been moved on to its line, and why, too, do so many of the fort gates open out beyond the wall-line? As with any frontier control, too, it is an admission of failure of communication. It marks the end of Roman dreams of expansion, though these still lingered on through part of the second century, and forms a crystallisation of the edges of the empire – a barrier to keep people in as well as out.

The short stretch of wall at Planetrees, about 1.5km (1 mile) east of Chesters

Despite this, it forms one of the most elaborate and complete groups of Roman sites and remains in the world, and was clearly the result of a massive input of energy and resources. Whether we should view it as an admirable achievement or as the Romans' own admission that their empire could not stretch forever must be left to the reader and the visitor.

The Wall at Chesters

The line chosen for the Wall involved crossing three major rivers, the North Tyne, the Irthing, and the Eden. At each of these there is a fort nearby, and Chesters Fort lies just west of the point where the Wall crosses the river North Tyne. From the east the Wall descends Brunton Bank following a straight course, difficult now to distinguish because of the tree-cover. There are two visible portions of

the Wall on this descent: the small fragment at Planetrees and the short stretch of wall with its accompanying turret at Brunton, Turret 26b. From Brunton Turret, the Wall dropped further down into the valley of the Tyne, passing the site of Milecastle 27 in open fields, before it reached the east abutment of the Roman bridge opposite Chesters Fort.

At its river crossing, Hadrian's Wall changed direction, turning a few degrees northwards to ascend Walwick bank, and then keeping to a straight line for nearly three miles west of Chesters before reaching Limestone Corner, the most northerly point on its line. The line it follows therefore originally cut straight through the middle of Chesters Fort, for, like several of the early series of forts added to the line of the Wall, Chesters sits astride it, with its northern third projecting beyond it and interrupting its course.

In the original planning for the Wall, when the siting of permanent forts on its line was not envisaged, Turret 27a (in its normal position, a third of a Roman mile west of Milecastle 27, on the other side of the River Tyne) should have stood on the spot now occupied by the fort itself. Excavation in 1945 was able to demonstrate that fragmentary traces of this turret, dismantled almost as soon as built, do in fact lie just east of the present headquarters building at the centre of the fort. This is revealing proof that Chesters was added to the line of the Wall at a secondary stage in the planning process.

The History of Chesters Fort

The name of the fort

The Roman names of the forts along Hadrian's Wall are found in several written sources. As far as Chesters is concerned, the main source is the *Notitia Dignitatum*, a late Roman list of the civilian and military posts within the imperial government. Under the command of the Duke of the British Provinces, and among a list of other postings 'along the line of the vallum', comes the Prefect of the Second Asturian Cavalry Wing, based at *Cilurnum*. Inscriptions attest the presence at Chesters of this cavalry troop from the end of the second century onwards, and the listing in the *Notitia* fits very well both with its position in the list (which progresses from east to west) and with known garrisons attested at other forts to its east. There is little doubt that the Roman name for this site was *Cilurnum*, which, if its derivation is from a Celtic root, may have something to do with a cauldron – perhaps a reference to a swirling pool of water within the Tyne nearby.

The fort garrison

Several of the Roman inscriptions found at Chesters attest the presence of a variety of troop units. An altar dedicated to the Disciplina of the Emperor Hadrian found in 1978 and now in the museum appears to give part of the name of the earliest garrison. This was a wing of cavalry – *ala Augusta ob virtutem appellate* – 'named "Augusta" on account of its valour'. This unit, if indeed that is its full name, is not attested elsewhere in Britain during the build-up to the construction of the Wall under Hadrian, though a unit of the same name appears later to have been stationed at Old Carlisle fort, in Cumbria: it is possible that its award for bravery was gained as a result of recent action in the north under Trajan. The inscription does confirm, however, that the fort had an early garrison of cavalry. The site, on level ground, with its three main gates beyond the Wall, was tactically suited to the deployment of a rapid strike force.

Little is known of the development of the fort during the second century, partly because what can now be seen was excavated in the middle and later years of the nineteenth century, when little attention was given to any but the most obvious phases of stone buildings. In fact the fort defences, the headquarters building and parts of the bath house appear to be the only original – that is Hadrianic – portions of the site which can now be seen and have been examined. The commandant's house and the barrack blocks now on view are later developments, and they conceal, buried beneath them, and still virtually untouched, further elements of the Hadrianic layout.

A chance find of a military discharge diploma, dated to AD146, and discovered on excavation in the east guardchamber of the south gate, suggests that by this date the garrison was no longer of cavalry. A diploma such as this was issued to an auxiliary (non-Roman) soldier on retirement from military service. It legalised his marriage, present or future, and granted both to him and any children he might subsequently bring up (but not to his wife) the privilege of Roman

The military discharge diploma, granting citizenship to a number of soldiers from British units, and dated AD146. It suggests that by this date Chesters was no longer manned by cavalry units but by British infantry.

citizenship. The Chesters diploma, a copy of which can be seen in the museum, is fragmentary, and does not reveal which unit was in garrison at the fort at the time, but strongly suggests that it was one of infantry.

A number of other inscriptions, some recording building work within the fort, attest the presence of troops either on detached duty or on permanent station. One, which cannot be dated, but which probably belongs to some point in the second century, records the First Cohort of Dalmatians, originally from the area of present-day Yugoslavia. This stone was found upside-down and re-used as one of the steps leading down to the underground strong room in the headquarters. Further fragments, also found re-used in later work, but probably belonging to the reign of Antoninus Pius (AD138–61), record legionary work-parties and may suggest a legionary detachment in occupation of the fort at a time when the Wall itself was largely abandoned. A further change of garrison is indicated by a tombstone which records the death of a daughter of a commanding officer of the First Cohort of Vangiones from the Upper Rhineland. If the daughter's name, Aurelia, had been chosen following the accession to the imperial throne of Marcus Aurelius in AD161, it shows that the Vangiones were at Chesters in the latter part of the second century.

By 184, a new unit was in post at Chesters, and one which seems to have stayed put for the remainder of the fort's active service. An inscription which records the provision of a water supply to the fort during the time that Ulpius Marcellus was governor of the province bears the name of the cavalry unit *Ala II Asturum*. The same unit is named on a carved relief which probably once had pride of place in the regimental 'chapel' in the headquarters. This depicts the standard bearer and records the regiment's loyalty to the reigning emperors (Elagabalus and Severus Alexander, AD221–2), before the name of the former was expunged from the records and had to be chipped off the inscription. The Asturian cavalry are found still in garrison at Chesters within the list of units recorded in the *Notitia Dignitatum*, a document which in its final form dates from no earlier than the end of the fourth century. There is thus no evidence for any further change in the occupancy of the fort.

The surviving part of an inscription set up by the Ala II Asturum. In the fragmentary lower portion is a depiction of the standard bearer's head, and a standard with the words 'Virtus Augg'– the virtue of the emperors. Note how one of the 'G's at the end of the word Augg in the top line has been obliterated after Elagabalus' memory was erased from the records.

The fort layout

Roman forts throughout the empire evolved to a similar if not absolutely standard pattern during the course of the first century AD. The temporary camp used by the army of the Roman Republic was described in the second century BC by the Greek writer Polybius, and already by that date it contained many of the elements of the fort plan which we have come to regard as typically Roman. By the third century AD, when Hyginus, writing a technical manual on surveying techniques, described a standard pattern for a Roman fortress, the layout was still substantially the same. Excavation has shown that although there are sometimes surprising deviations from this overall design, by the time of Hadrian the planning and layout of a fort had reached something of a standard form with relatively minor variations.

In plan the fort would normally look in outline like a playing card, rectangular with rounded corners, and approximately half as long as it was broad. The walls were normally of stone, though they could be of turf-and-timber, and were surrounded by at least one V-shaped ditch running parallel to them. Midway along each of the short sides there would be a double-portalled entrance. The main gates in the two longer sides would be about a third of the distance along them, at opposite ends of a street running through the fort. This left space for a subsidiary entrance, where this was needed, equidistant between this gate and the far end.

The fort walls were backed on the inside by a rampart of earth which was interrupted by towers projecting within the fort at the rounded corners and at intervals between them and the gates. The rampart area might on occasion be used for bakehouses, workshops and latrines, and was separated from the remainder of the buildings within the fort by a road which ran round the whole circuit.

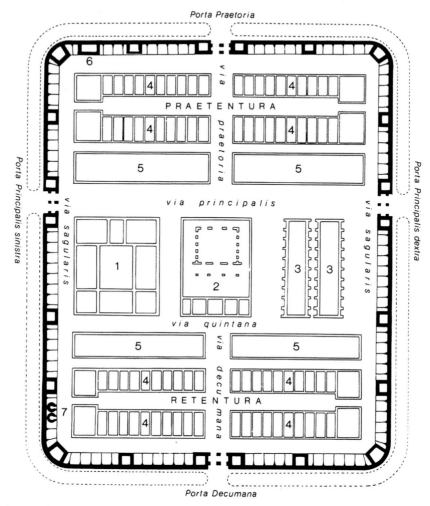

The layout of an 'idealised' Roman fort, based on elements from several of the forts on Hadrian's Wall and elsewhere. 1 – Commandant's house; 2 – Headquarters building; 3 – Granaries or storehouses; 4 – Barrack blocks; 5 – Stables or workshops; 6 – Latrines; 7 – Ovens (often associated with bakehouses).

At the junction of the two main roads within the fort lay the entrance to the headquarters building (*principia*), which interrupted the line of the fort's long axis, and occupied the central third of the fort. Within the remainder of this central strip lay other administrative buildings – stores depots for food or weapons, workshops,

or perhaps a hospital – and a space next to the headquarters was normally reserved for a relatively expansive house for the unit's commanding officer, normally of courtyard plan, and containing its own heating system and baths.

The remainder of the fort, the front and back portions (the fort was always

Reconstructed view looking down the alley between the pair of barrack blocks in the northern part of the fort. The men's mess rooms open off under the colonnaded section, and the wider centurion's quarters are at the end of the building. At the end of the alley is one of the towers attached to the fort wall. (Drawing by Peter Connolly)

assumed to be 'facing' the enemy with the majority of its gates issuing forwards), was filled with accommodation for the troops, for their mounts (if they were cavalry) or for baggage animals. The type of unit in garrison would in theory be reflected in the size and number of the barrack blocks contained within the fort. If it was an auxiliary cohort, for example, there would have been a paper strength of 480 men, divided into six *centuriae*, centuries, thus requiring six barrack blocks; if it were a cavalry wing (*ala*), there would be 512 men, divided into 16 *turmae* (squadrons) of 32 men each, two of which might be accommodated within each barrack block, thus requiring eight. However, the exercise of determining what sort of ground plan was actually required for particular units is fraught with difficulties. The picture is complicated both by the existence within the Roman army of

almost double size units, or mixed units of cavalry and infantry; and by our own lack of detailed knowledge about the numbers of horses attached to individual units, or about what structural changes (some of them perhaps internal partitioning only within barrack blocks) were the norm when a fort was taken over by a new garrison of different type from the one before.

In general, however, although barracks, stables and store-buildings are all usually long, narrow buildings, the first can normally be distinguished by the provision, at their rampart end, of a suite of more comfortable domestic rooms for what would nowadays be called the NCO – the centurion of an infantry unit or the decurion if cavalry. Here he might have had his own kitchen and latrine as well as separate living and sleeping accommodation.

Portrait of John Clayton, owner of the Chesters estate from 1832 onwards. The portrait is in Chesters Museum.

The Chesters Estate and John Clayton

Brief descriptions of Chesters figure in several antiquarian accounts of travels in the Wall area from the sixteenth and seventeenth century onwards, though these afford little detail and do no more than whet the appetite for what could then still be seen. One eighteenth-century visitor recorded that Chesters was 'the first station in my tour where the direct appearance of regular streets was observed', and described the fort's interior as crowded with the remains of stone buildings.

The Chesters Estate was purchased in 1796 by Nathaniel Clayton who, in forming a parkland setting for his country house, levelled and grassed over most of the visible remains of the Roman fort which lay between it and the Tyne. In the process, he made a collection of a number of antiquities which came to light, but there is no other evidence that he took a great deal of interest in the Roman site on his doorstep.

His son John, however, who succeeded to the property in 1832, took a passionate interest not only in the fort of Chesters and its immediate surroundings, but also in Roman remains in the neighbourhood. Up until his death in 1890, much of his spare time was devoted to excavating and protecting the remains of the Roman Wall – at the time of his death he had acquired five of the major Roman sites in the area in order to secure their preservation – as well as to enhancing the collection of antiquities from many different sites which is still housed at Chesters.

John Clayton's excavations were directed at the exploration of many of the better known sites on the Wall. These included the investigation of parts of the forts or their surrounding buildings at Housesteads (1849 onwards)

This kind of basic layout is reflected in the plan of Chesters. The fort faced north, and the forward part of the fort, with its three main double-portalled gates, faced the direction from which attack was expected and through which retribution would sally forth. The complete fort plan, however, is not at present exposed at the site, and additions and alterations during the course of its long occupation have in any case blurred the crisp edges of the original Hadrianic plan. This must have been the case with many of the sites, on Hadrian's Wall as elsewhere, which were under occupation for almost two and a half centuries. At Chesters, however, it is none the less possible to appreciate the fort design which is so recognisable a feature of the Roman army, and so clearly a sign of the Roman occupation of parts of Africa and the near East as well as widespread parts of Europe.

These two photographs by J P Gibson were taken in 1885 and 1886, and show the progress of excavation work in the bath house between those dates. Photographs such as these, preserved in the collections of the Northumberland Record Office, are valuable evidence of the extent of work on the site in early excavations. (Reproduced by kind permission of the Gibson family, via Mr J Gibson and Northumberland Record Office)

Carrawburgh (1873-76), and Carvoran (1886). He also instigated excavation work at the milecastles of Cawfields in 1848 and Housesteads in 1853, as well as at Turret 29a (Black Carts). One of the most spectacular finds was that of the well of Coventina at Carrawburgh, where excavation began in 1876. In achieving so much, Clayton, who reportedly devoted only the Mondays of each week to his practical archaeological activities, was assisted by William Tailford, father and son, on whom fell much of the responsibility for these relatively widespread campaigns of work, including the examination of the fort and surroundings of Chesters itself.

Virtually all that can be seen of the fort of Chesters today, including the remains of the Roman bridge across the Tyne, was the product of work instigated by John Clayton. His publication of the results was not as complete as might have been desired, but the papers which he did write to describe his discoveries are supplemented by a number of plans of the site prepared for successive editions of *The Roman Wall*, first published in 1851 by John Collingwood Bruce. From these it is

clear that Clayton's work at Chesters was not confined only to those parts of the site visible today, and that certain structures were backfilled after their discovery.

Clayton himself was responsible for establishing Chesters as an archaeological site with remains which could be inspected by visitors. Within the estate there was a small garden pavilion in which some of the more notable finds – from

The museum at Chesters, built in 1896 to house the collections built up by John Clayton from Chesters and elsewhere

Watercolour painting by David Mossman, dating from about 1860. This shows the excavation of the eastern bridge abutment in progress. Note the impression of submerged bridge piers in the water, and the size of the massive abutment in relation to the figure standing on it. (Tullie House City Museum and Art Gallery, Carlisle)

Chesters and elsewhere – were displayed. At his death in 1890, some attempts were made to catalogue these and to establish with as much accuracy as was then possible where they had originally come from. Nathaniel Clayton commissioned and had built the permanent museum to house the antiquities. Completed in 1896, the collection it contains and the way it is presented have remained virtually unaltered to the present day, retaining a spirit and period flavour of which John Clayton would doubtless have approved.

In 1954, the remains of the fort and a small portion of the settlement including the bath house were placed in the guardianship of the Ministry of Works. As successor to that body, English Heritage now cares

for the remains, and also leases and administers the museum, which has its own independent body of trustees.